I Am
DAILY ATTUNEMENT

A guide to self-healing and attuning to the Higher Consciousness

Author:
Barbara Ann Strassman

Content

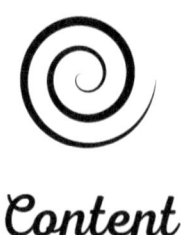

PREFACE

INTRODUCTION

PART I   Reconnect and Resurrect Your True Self – A Pathway to Self-Healing from the Ground Up

           CHAPTER 1 - Trauma: Who or What Took Your Breath Away? Reconnect Through Your Breath

           CHAPTER 2 - Setting the Stage

           CHAPTER 3 - Reconnect to Your True–Self & Light Body
- *Level One: Just Breathe*
- *Level Two: Equal Breath*
- *Level Three: Grounding and Connecting to Heaven and Earth*
- *Level Four: Violet Flame Cleansing and Self-Healing*
- *Level Five: Balance the Divine Masculine and Divine Feminine Rays*
- *Level Six: I AM THAT I AM*

PART II   Realign and Redesign to Your Divine Blueprint

           Chapter 4 - Tools for Self Healing

           Chapter 5 - Redesign Your Life

REFERENCES

Preface

I recently made a sacred pilgrimage to South India with a group of beautiful, like-minded souls. My experience was that the journey was divinely orchestrated as an Ascension process. I experienced a raising of my vibration and a raising of my consciousness with each sacred site we visited. Immersive it was on so many levels that I am still processing and assimilating all that I experienced these many months later.

Over the course of 14 days I was blessed with many "messages" and visions, which I am truly grateful for. The last sacred site was in Tiruvannamalai. Our first stop was the Ashram of Sri Ramana Maharshi where we had time to meditate and visit the samadhi shrine of Ramana Maharshi. On the second day we climbed up a small portion of Mount Arunachala to meditate in some of the sacred caves where Ramana lived and meditated for some 54 years. While meditating in the first sacred cave, he came to me and said, "Sacred and Holy you shall be." I saw myself, barefoot, dressed all in white, standing at the entrance of my healing center. My hands folded in prayer pose and eyes closed, looking so serene, in a state of devotion. The walls were all white with accents and trims of gold. Indian tapestries were hanging on the walls. Then I saw his face in a cloud above me. It seemed the cloud was the smoke of the fire of the mountain. He is One with Shiva!

Stunned by this verbal and visual message, it reminded me of a divine encounter a few days earlier while staying at the Saccidananda Ashram. There I received several messages from deceased Father Bede Griffiths who was a beloved spiritual friend of our dear spiritual group leader, Andrew Harvey. One message was that he would inform Andrew of something, for me. Well, on the last day of the trip as we left Tiruvannamalai I sat with Andrew and out of nowhere he very directly listed several things I needed to do for humanity!

One message was actually similar to that of Sri Ramana, in that I am to live in that higher state of consciousness that I attain when facilitating healing sessions. I am to live in that higher state of consciousness all the time, all day, every day.

The next instruction was that I am to create four videos to help humanity get back to the basics and to learn to Self-Heal. Humanity needs to become more grounded, more centered and we all need to learn how to work with the breath, the breath that connects us back to Source! I was told that the way I so easily connect to the divine with the breath, is what humanity needs to learn and it is so important for all humanity to understand that this divine connection is possible! It is easy! Humanity needs help, Andrew kept stressing.

Then he told me that I am to write a book teaching all this that will go along with the videos--a small, simple book to help us heal ourselves. We need the basics so we can get back on track, feel safe, move forward, heal ourselves and save the world. That book is what you are reading now.

Andrew also said I am to share 11 quotes on "Birthing the Divine Human" on my website. As, ultimately, this is a Journey to Self – Self Realization. The breath is the KEY and the KEY is within us, within our heart.

I listened intently to all Andrew instructed me to do, and all is being done as I believe it was asked of me. I ask you to listen deeply, too, for the message was for you, for humanity, for we are ALL ONE.

Introduction

"Know that all strength, all healing of every nature is the changing of the vibrations from within – the ATTUNING of the divine within the living tissue of a body to Creative Energies. This alone is healing."

(1967-1) Edgar Cayce reading, The Sleeping Prophet

The journey within is as simple as a deep inhale and exhale, with focused attention, desire and adoration.

Inhale – rise and receive – the breath of Life
Exhale - shine and share – the gift of Life
Inhale – reconnect and resurrect
Exhale – realign and redesign

Four equal breaths. Four steps to birthing your true, divine Self. The number four represents stability. Four represents support, the four directions, four corners of the earth, and it is said to represent creation for on the fourth day God created the Sun and the Moon.

The Equal Breath Practice is simply four breaths of equal length. Giving your Self--your True Self--a few moments of undivided attention at the start of each day is an invaluable tool in your search for inner peace. This is the easiest process of connecting to Higher Consciousness and it is most assuredly a tool of transformation.

The breath takes us back to the beginning of creation. The Divine Breath, the gift of Life, in each moment can take us back to the moment of creation, to our connection with Higher Consciousness from which we sprang. Our powerful breath can flush out thoughts that clutter our mind, and aid in eliminating worry, fear and anxiety. The breath is a key step in reconnecting to our True Self, to the life we truly desire to live, bringing ourselves back into balance, stability, harmony and inner peace.

I invite you now to inhale deeply, then exhale and flush out the thoughts that clutter your mind. Let go of your monkey mind, let go of fear, worry and anxiety and CHOOSE to experience this powerful tool that brought us all into life. It is as easy as one, two, three, four. Four steps to rise and shine! Shine your Light from Within!

I will also share other tools for living in the present moment, assistance for empaths, and for choosing happiness.

Rise and receive, shine and share, is just another way of saying receiving and giving, as you align with the breath of the Divine throughout each day, effortlessly experiencing the miracle of living fully in the moment.

You are the healer! Choose to heal yourself and then together we can heal the world!

∽

Before you embark on this journey, may I invite you to allow for the POSSIBILITY of being fully engaged, consciously engaged with life, each and every moment? In this process you will be opening your mind to the Realms of Illumined Truth, elevating your consciousness and experiencing life from a higher perspective. Let me share with you some additional POSSIBILITIES of the magical and mystical end result!

* Calmness, clarity, peace and serenity.

* Being grounded, rooted, AND connected with your Higher Consciousness, which assists you in staying centered and more even-keeled, no matter what energies life sends your way.

* Awareness that life does not just happen to you; you are part of the happening!

* In moments of stress or anxiety, you rise above the situation with your sacred breath and consciously choose to respond from a higher vibration, a higher awareness.

* Awakening-- how you CHOOSE to respond to life and to all living things-- affects yourself and all humanity.

* Your energy field is expanding and a higher vibratory rate is achieved.

*Your physical body as well as the four lower bodies come to vibrate in a state of perfect health.

* You are HIGH on Life!

* A "knowing" that ALL is just as it is meant to be.

* Expanding to fields of consciousness that connect you to the Divine Mind, the Collective Consciousness, to the Christ Consciousness.

(Please note that the Christ Consciousness is a state of Being, a state of Higher Consciousness, not about a specific person. Many great gurus, saints and masters have achieved this state of Being.)

God gave us FREE WILL. Let's use it to our benefit and thus to the benefit of humanity! It is this easy to start and come together – One Breath, One Mind, One heartbeat! WE ARE ALL ONE!

Videos to accompany the book:

To help in your Daily Attunement process, I have created videos to accompany the exercises written in this book. The step-by-step, simple instructions guide you at your own pace to a deeper awareness of body, mind and spirit. Once that beautiful connection has been made and you are in tune and flowing with the process, I offer an added bonus of six guided breath meditations in which the vibration takes you even deeper because they are partially guided by Angelic Beings. (Levels 4, 5 and 6 are all on one video.)

I also have included videos of sacred mantras to help you access the Higher Consciousness. Ground yourselves deeply, so that you may rise high!

Scan the QR Code below with the camera on your phone to access the videos.

Journal pages:

After each Attunement Level, I have included some sample journal pages. A journal is most helpful to increase your awareness, which is why I encourage you to journal on the questions I provide. You can use the pages provided within, or use your own journal.

Part 1

Chapter 1

Trauma: Who or what took your breath away?

Have you ever noticed that your breath is shallow? Have you ever felt a tightness or constriction in your chest? Have you ever caught yourself holding your breath?

Believe it or not, my experience with healing work is that very often it is about reconnecting to our breath. Someone or something took our breath away, i.e.; knocked the wind out of us. When I ask "body" this question, a memory will surface. Who or what can be a person that did cause physical harm to you, or it could be an event that shocked you and took your breath away. It can be a physical body event or an energy body event, including the emotional body. The feeling of being "sucker punched" sometimes arises. With harsh or hurtful words, someone hit us in the gut! There are all types of "traumas" that can take our breath away. They can even occur in utero! Thus the need to "call back our breath".

My experience is we need to acknowledge that we are also calling back the lost parts of Self, the parts that have disconnected / disassociated due to the traumatic event. We are reconnecting to Self, reconnecting to all parts of Self that we may become whole again. Then the resurrection process begins. We pick ourselves back up, we rise up and we shine once again with the wholeness of our divine being.

The breath helps us to connect to the higher consciousness and I say we Reconnect and Resurrect our true Self. When we breathe in and reach our focus up to the higher realms, we are breathing in the energy of Source, God! When we exhale we are sending it through and out to humanity. We are reconnecting to Source, to

God, to Higher Consciousness and bringing ourselves back to life!

Sometimes the trauma becomes stuck in our body, in our diaphragmatic region, and we need hands-on healing assistance to remove the trauma and to call back our life force, our breath. Clearing the so-called trauma from the cells, from the tissue, is important for true healing and letting go, and Resurrecting ourselves. We have tissue memory, muscle memory and any time there is a feeling that is similar to the trauma, our body can be re-triggered. The body may constrict further, breath tightens further, emotions heighten and our energy flow is impacted, as well as organs and glands over time.

Trauma causes disconnection from ourselves, from loved ones and from Source. The region of the diaphragm is the third chakra which is related to our sense of Self, our self-esteem and how we see ourselves fitting into the world. It is time for humanity to release the traumas, to call back their breath, their life force and to Reconnect and Resurrect themselves back to full life!

So are you ready to start your part in Self-Healing? You owe it to yourself and all your loved ones.

Chapter 2

Setting the Stage

Where might you find a quiet space, within your home, where you can slide upon the rhythm of your breath into your heart? Creating a space that is sacred and holy to you assists in the "dropping in", into Self. I invite you to feel out the space that is right for you and where you will be undisturbed. A sacred space may contain objects that carry a vibration that resonates as sacred and holy, such as:

Crystals carry a variety of vibrations that may assist in divine connection and healing. Clear quartz especially assists in connecting with Higher Consciousness.

Statues of Ascended Beings, Saints, gurus, religious figures that hold meaning for you.

Pictures of the above entities, or pictures of the beauty of Nature, or what God or Universe means to you, of serenity , of love, of Divine Connection.

Incense burning helps to clear the energies of the room and provide a sense of calm.

Candles burning may release scents that may have a calming effect or an uplifting effect. Candles also are a tool to focus upon, stilling the mind.

Sense what objects and images help you connect to the Divine, to Source, or to nature, objects that resonate for you and within you. This may change as your vibration rises with the practices listed.

Imagery and scents are important for some folks, and sound is more important for others. You may wish to incorporate soft sacred music such as chants, gongs, or singing bowls, to set the mood for your Daily Attunement. Separately, experiences of Gong Baths/Singing bowls are a powerful release and cleansing of your light body and cellular body.

Lastly, help others respect your sacred space by having a visible sign of no disturbances, quiet, and no cell phones. This is a must. Tranquility at last!

Chapter 3

Reconnect To Your True-Self & Light Body

In my Divine Matrix healing work the first phase is to Reconnect and Resurrect. What are we reconnecting to? As we are energy, not just our physical bodies, you may surmise we are reconnecting to our energy bodies, our light bodies.

Many of you may have experienced **acupuncture** and know of the meridians. The meridians are lines of energy, known as Qi, that are accessed with needles placed in the acupuncture points to help circulate the Qi.

Reiki is a popular healing technique that works to cleanse and balance your aura and the chakras – spinning vortexes of energy that correspond to your physical body's endocrine system.

Reflexology is pressure applied with thumbs or fingers to nerve endings of the feet primarily, balancing the flow in all systems of the body. The nervous system, the chakras, the organs and glands, the cerebral spinal fluid and the overall energy systems of the body are stimulated, bringing the body back into a state of balance/homeostasis.

Craniosacral is another healing modality that works with the energy flow of your cerebral spinal fluid and **chiropractic** care is about the spine, the nervous system, subluxations and the energies that impact that system.

I equate these different energy modes with the electrical system in our house. We need all circuits working, we need to be plugged into the source of energy and we need to turn the Light(s) on!

These different energy systems will be positively impacted with our Daily Attunement exercises.

The Daily Attunement is a tool to assist in clearing energy flow blockages or stagnation, to assist energy centers like the chakras to be balanced, and assist areas of disconnect to be reconnected. Ultimately we are Reconnected with our True-Self, our Divine Self, remembering who we really are and thus we are coming alive again, we are Resurrecting our Divine Self and coming back to living life fully!

Daily Attunement Steps & Journal Prompts

Daily Attunement: Level 1

This Daily Attunement practice will create the possibility of living a more stable and more fluid life. When grounded and aligned you find that you handle life's ups and downs with more grace and ease. Your breath will become a tool of true transformation. How often do we say, "Just stop and breathe"? The breath is like a reset button and it helps you to choose how to better respond to difficult situations. Once you have integrated these steps into your life they become automatic in times of need and you will simply need just ONE in breath, hold and ONE out breath, to connect to the Higher-Divine Consciousness.

In the process of attuning to the Higher-Divine Consciousness and honoring our Sacred Self, a pose of alignment can be any of the following; a) standing straight and tall, b) sitting in a yogi, crossed legged position, c) sitting with feet flat on the ground and a straight spine, or d) lying supine.

Having said that, my experience is that feet flat on the floor often helps one visualize the flow of energy into Mother Earth, assisting us in the important process of rooting, grounding deep within the Divine Feminine. Laying down often brings us into a state of sleep which is not the intent.

Through these Daily Attunements you have the opportunity to experience the beginnings of Reconnection and Resurrection of your True Divine Self.

Scan the code below to use the accompanying videos to guide you through the practices.

Let's begin.

1. Stop, close your eyes, focusing deep within…or gazing deep within.

Then BE Still, breathe.

2. Notice your breath. Notice the sensations as you inhale through the nose and as you exhale out the mouth.

3. As you continue to breathe, notice your body as the breath becomes rhythmic and natural.

This is pretty easy, you CAN do it!

4. Did you hear or feel something, somewhere in your body? Was that your body communicating something to you?

Breathe, BE Still, and listen to that "something."

5. Was it a quiet voice within? Was it a body part calling for your attention? Listen closely as you float upon your breath, floating in between the empty spaces inside your body. Be still.

6. Deepen the awareness of breath. Deepen the listening, attune to body.

7. If the body is still calling for your attention, send the breath to that body part. Love it, breathe into it, be present with all that it is telling you. As you give the love and focus to this body part you may start to notice that the need for attention diminishes.

8. Notice the softening, inside and outside. Notice the serenity, the quiet, the peacefulness.

9. When fully relaxed and at peace, slowly open your eyes, wiggle your toes and fingers and bring your awareness back to your space.

Set the intention to carry these sensations and feelings with you throughout the day!

Anytime during the day that you feel a shift occurring, stop and breathe.

YOU'VE GOT THIS!

HAVE A BEAUTIFUL DAY!

I invite you to practice this for seven to 14 straight days before continuing to the next step.

One note, please be sure your inhale is deep and the exhale is powerful, audible. Your lungs should be expanding and contracting noticeably. When you inhale the belly goes out and when you exhale the belly goes back towards the spine.

The deepening of our connection to God/ Source , never ends so when these journal pages are filled please continue with a journal special to you.

Journal - Day 1

I **notice** in the beginning: _____

_____

I **notice** at the end: _____

_____

I **sense** in the beginning: _____

_____

I **sense** at the end: _____

_____

I **feel** in the beginning: _____

_____

I **feel** at the end: _____

_____

In the beginning my breath is: _____

At the end my breath is: _____

My diaphragm feels: _____

The biggest change I notice is: _____

_____

_____

Journal - Day 1

Journal - Day 2

I **notice** in the beginning: _____

_____

I **notice** at the end: _____

_____

I **sense** in the beginning: _____

_____

I **sense** at the end: _____

_____

I **feel** in the beginning: _____

_____

I **feel** at the end: _____

_____

In the beginning my breath is: _____

At the end my breath is: _____

My diaphragm feels: _____

The biggest change I notice is: _____

_____

_____

Journal - Day 2

Journal - Day 3

I **notice** in the beginning: _____
_____

I **notice** at the end: _____
_____

I **sense** in the beginning: _____
_____

I **sense** at the end: _____
_____

I **feel** in the beginning: _____
_____

I **feel** at the end: _____
_____

In the beginning my breath is: _____

At the end my breath is: _____

My diaphragm feels: _____

The biggest change I notice is: _____
_____
_____

Journal - Day 3

Daily Attunement: Level 2

You might be thinking, "Of course I breathe every day, this is silly!" "Of course I feel my body, this is childish!" Or maybe you are already realizing we often stop breathing!

We often have a very shallow breath, especially if we are anxious or tense. We hold our breath and lock our jaw and we don't even know it.

Is your diaphragm muscle working extra hard, or is it feeling tight and restricted? The diaphragm ideally contracts rhythmically and continually. Can you feel the sensations of the diaphragm as you focus on your breath? No need to feel silly, we are all One!

"Being a person requires that one stop their frantic 'doing' and take time out to 'breathe' and to 'feel'. If one has the courage to accept and 'feel' the pain, sadness, and inner emptiness in one's life, one can heal trauma and gain pleasure, fulfillment, and joy."

-Alexander Lowen, M.D. "Fear of Life"

1. Stop, close your eyes, focusing deep within...or gazing deep within.

Then BE Still, breathe.

2. Notice your breath. Notice the sensations as you inhale through the nose and as you exhale out the mouth.

3. As you continue to breathe, notice your body as the breath becomes rhythmic and natural.

4. Did you hear or feel something, somewhere in your body? Was that your body communicating something to you? Breathe, BE Still and listen to that "something." Was it a quiet voice within? Was it a body part calling for your attention? Listen closely as you float upon your breath, floating in between the empty spaces inside your body. Be still.

5. Deepen the awareness of breath. Deepen the listening, attune to body. Notice if the body is still calling for your attention and send your breath to that body part. Love it, breathe into it, be present with all that it is telling you. As you give the love and focus to this body part you may start to notice that the need for attention diminishes.

6. Notice the softening, inside and outside.

7. Notice the serenity, the quiet, the peacefulness.

8. I invite you now to create a breathing pattern that will interrupt the stress patterns in your brain. As you inhale, count until the breath is full. Then hold the inhale for the same number of counts. Then exhale through the mouth for the same number of counts. Then leave the exhale out for the same number of counts.

Example: If you inhale to the count of four, then hold the breath for the count of four, exhale to the count of 4 and leave the breath out for a count of four. Then start over again with the inhale and each part for the same count of four. If the count of four is comfortable at each step then continue for 15 repetitions. If it is not comfortable, then try a higher or lower count until you find the count that is right for you. You may choose a three count or possibly higher, a five count. Then continue for 15 repetitions.

In the beginning you are thinking and counting until suddenly it all comes together and you let go and naturally float into bliss.

9. Continue the equal breath with the count that feels most comfortable, for 15 rounds.

10. The breath, the breath of God/Source/Universe, the breath of Life. The breath speaks: Be Still and Know that I AM GOD. Stay in this knowing for as long as it feels right.

11. I invite you to do this practice ideally twice a day, morning and at bedtime. Starting the day calm and serene helps us to handle the daily events differently. Ending the day helps us obtain a restful and restorative sleep. It is even more beneficial if you can comfortably intertwine this routine somewhere in the middle of your day also, as a fulcrum point.

12. At the end of seven days, notice the changes in your breathing practice and the changes in how you handle your daily stress. Notice if your mind is operating differently and make a note of how so.

This will become so routine someday that you will be able to JUST DO IT – with one round of an inhale, hold, exhale and BE!

Dr. Herbert Benson, founder of Mind/Body Medical Institute at Massachusetts General Hospital in Boston, developed the Equal Breath Practice.

Journal

At the end of the 7 days:

My diaphragm feels: _____

_____

My equal breath count is: _____

My mind now is: _____

_____

I notice: _____

_____

I sense: _____

_____

I feel: _____

_____

I drop into my Daily Attunement easier each day: YES   NO

The equal breath has become routine: YES   NO

I am using the equal breath in moments of stress: YES   NO

I am more aware of my breath in my daily activities: YES   NO

I am less stressed: YES   NO

Journal

Daily Attunement: Level 3

If you have not started the journal I again invite you to do so. Just noting changes helps keep us attuned. Anything and everything that comes to you belongs in the journal. Life happens so quickly that we miss a lot and forget a lot. I have listed some suggestions to journal about as the journal helps us to see how far we have come.

Consider even journaling comments people make, as by now those close to you may be noticing a difference. They may not have clarity on what is different but they sense the changes within you. This is great as you are always affecting them, even if they don't know it. Sooner or later they will ask you, "What is different? What are you doing differently?" Then the dynamic, powerful sharing begins! Wow, you are having a positive impact on others without even trying!

In Level Three we expand our vibrational field and we must be truly grounded to achieve a state of balance, centeredness and serenity.

Standing often helps the grounding process and visualizing the energy really going into the center of the earth from the bottom of our feet. Also, standing and lifting your arms up to the sky, with fingers pointed straight up to the sky, is inviting the energy to pour in and through and into your heart center. Invoke the Divine and the Divine responds.

It is this easy, as I stated before. One day as I was sitting in an airport I heard, "Just tell them to put their arms up to the sky and breathe! That is all they need to connect to the Divine. It is easy, just do it."

1. Stop, close your eyes, focusing deep within...or gazing deep within.

Then BE Still, breathe.

2. Notice your breath. Notice the sensations as you inhale through the nose and as you exhale out the mouth.

3. As you continue to breathe, notice your body once the breath has become rhythmic and natural.

4. Did you hear or feel something, somewhere in your body? Was that your body communicating something to you? Breathe, BE Still, and listen to that something. Was it a quiet voice within? Was it a body part calling for your attention? Listen closely as you float upon your breath, floating in between the empty spaces inside your body. BE still.

5. Deepen the awareness of breath. Deepen the listening, attune to body. Notice if the body is still calling for your attention and then send the breath to that body part. Love it, breathe into it, be present with all that it is telling you. As you give the love and focus to this body part you may start to notice that the need for attention diminishes.

6. Notice the softening, inside and outside.

7. Notice the serenity, the quiet, the peacefulness.

8. I invite you now to create a breathing pattern that will interrupt the stress patterns in your brain. As you inhale, count until the breath feels full . Then hold the inhale for the same number of counts. Then exhale through the mouth for the same number of counts. Then leave the exhale out for the same number of counts.

Example: If you inhale to the count of four, then hold the breath for the count of four, exhale to the count of four and leave the breath out for the count of four. Then start over again with the inhale and each part for the same count of four. If the count of four is comfortable at each step then continue for 15 repetitions. If it is not comfortable, then try a higher or lower count until you find the count that is right for you. You may choose a three count or possibly higher, a five count.

9. Continue the equal breath with the count that is most comfortable for 15 rounds.

10. The breath, the breath of God/Source/Universe, the breath of Life. The breath speaks: Be Still and Know that I AM GOD. Stay in this KNOWING for as long as feels right.

11. Now, in this state of grace, of equal breath, please raise your arms straight up to the sky, reaching up to heaven! Inhale deeply and exhale deeply as you say, "Good Morning God! I AM HERE!" (I recommend you say this out loud for more power, power of the spoken word and I feel it is important to do this and the following steps standing.)

12. Visualize the Pure River of Life. The Pure River is God's Light and Love flowing down into your fingertips, down through your arms and into your heart. Notice sensations in the fingers, in your hands, and into your arms.

13. Visualize this river of God's Light and Love also flowing with your breath down into your Crown chakra and gently, slowly flowing down through each of the chakra centers, through the center of your body and all the way through to the base of your spine.

14. Your breath is like a lazy river flowing through the whole body. Flowing gently, smoothly, and rhythmically. You are becoming one with the pure river of spiritual love. In this sense of Oneness your heart expands and you are radiating this love within yourself and outside of yourself to others, to humanity. Love heals.

15. Noticing, sensing, breathing. Deep within the body, notice the sensations, notice the flow, feel the vibration of love expanding.

Love heals. Love will save mankind. Radiating love, going with the flow of life, of love.

16. See your body filled with sparkles of Light. Notice, sense the sparkles, within the body.

17. Notice, sense the energy of love, caring, attention to/for you. Allow yourself to FEEL.

18. The River continues to flow. Allow this beautiful light and love to flow from the base of your spine, into each leg and down through into your feet. The light and love may also run between your legs into the space between your feet. Notice the sensations.

19. Then from the soles of your feet it flows into the center of the Earth, our Divine Mother. As the light continues to flow even deeper you realize you are like a beautiful tree growing roots, down, down, down into the center of the earth. Notice the sensations as the energy goes deep into the earth. Love is emanating all around you.

20. Visualize the energy rooting, grounding, or anchoring into the center of your Divine Mother. To the front, to the back, to the right, to the left you are fully rooted and grounded, fully connected with the healing energy of Divine Mother. Notice, sense all the roots in all directions.

21. Feeling so connected to the Earth and alive with the energy of the light and love from above, soak in this energy, absorbing Divine Mother Earth's beloved nurturance, her support, her creativity. Now sense and see a green light of healing energy flowing upwards! Inhale the green light, the divine energy up and into the soles of your feet. Notice the sensations as it rises.

22. With each inhalation you are bringing the energy up into each leg, into the base of your spine and up through each chakra, up through the center of your body and all the way up to your Crown chakra. Notice, sense the vibration of your whole body!

23. With the fullness of your desire, the fullness of your deepest intentions, send this green healing light up, from the crown

chakra up into the heavens, up to Source, up to the Great Central Sun, about 12 or so inches above your head. The Great Central Sun is a golden yellow ball of light like our sun.

24. Visualize your hands encircling, enfolding the Great Central Sun with the energy of Divine Mother. Feel the deep connection, as if your hands/fingers were roots growing around the sun. Notice, sense, the energies in your hands and arms as you embrace, and root into this golden sun.

25. KNOW you are now fully rooted and anchored to Heaven and Earth. You are a vessel, a channel of love and light between Heaven and Earth. You are the channel through which God's Light and Love reaches Humanity. Balanced, grounded, and connected. Be Still, here and now.

26. BE the vessel, BE the channel, Just BE. BE still and Know that I AM GOD.

27. Continue this process from step 11 through 26, six more times. Six is the number of manifestation. You ARE a Divine Channel between your Father/Mother God, between heaven and earth. You ARE a channel of God's Light and Love.

28. When you are feeling complete, whole and balanced, slowly bring your focus back to the room, and your body. Wiggle your toes, fingers, take a few deep breaths and slowly start to open your eyes. Notice your whole Being.

29. BE Still.

30. Give thanks to your I AM Presence, to God/Source, to the angelic kingdom.

I invite you to bask in this illuminated River of Light for as many weeks/months as you know to be right for you. This is sacred territory, a sacred communion if you will, communion of the deepest level.

Journal - Day 1

I feel the love: YES NO

My diaphragm feels: _____

_____

My equal breath count is: _____

My mind now is: _____

_____

I notice: _____

_____

I sense: _____

_____

I feel: _____

_____

I drop into my Daily Attunement easier each day: YES NO

The equal breath has become routine: YES NO

I am conscious of the energies/feelings/emotions of the day: YES NO

I am more aware of my breath in my daily activities: YES NO

I am less stressed: YES NO

Emotions (e- energy in motion) are arising as I am more aware of my body and breath. The buried emotions are arising and I feel:

Sad   Happy   Frustrated   Angry   Blissful   Misunderstood   Worried   Confused   Lost   Ignored   Grateful   Overwhelmed   Insecure

Journal - Day 1

Journal your emotions fully:

_____

_____

_____

_____

_____

_____

_____

_____

_____

_____

I feel rooted/grounded: YES NO

I notice sensations in the fingers/hands: YES NO

I can visualize the Golden Light: YES NO

I can visualize the green light: YES NO

I can feel/sense the Light going through my body: YES NO

I sense the energy of Divine Love or: _____

I sense a feeling that is new to me that I cannot name: YES NO

I feel: _____

_____

I AM enjoying life more FULLY!: YES NO

Journal - Day 1

Journal - Day 1

Journal - Day 2

I feel the love: YES NO

My diaphragm feels: _____

_____

My equal breath count is: _____

My mind now is: _____

_____

I notice: _____

_____

I sense: _____

_____

I feel: _____

_____

I drop into my Daily Attunement easier each day: YES NO

The equal breath has become routine: YES NO

I am conscious of the energies/feelings/emotions of the day: YES NO

I am more aware of my breath in my daily activities: YES NO

I am less stressed: YES NO

Emotions (e- energy in motion) are arising as I am more aware of my body and breath. The buried emotions are arising and I feel:

Sad Happy Frustrated Angry Blissful Misunderstood Worried Confused Lost Ignored Grateful Overwhelmed Insecure

Journal - Day 2

Journal your emotions fully:

_____
_____
_____
_____
_____
_____
_____
_____
_____
_____

I feel rooted/grounded: YES   NO

I notice sensations in the fingers/hands: YES   NO

I can visualize the Golden Light: YES   NO

I can visualize the green light: YES   NO

I can feel/sense the Light going through my body: YES   NO

I sense the energy of Divine Love or: _____

I sense a feeling that is new to me that I cannot name: YES   NO

I feel: _____

_____

I AM enjoying life more FULLY!: YES   NO

Journal - Day 2

Journal - Day 2

Journal - Day 3

I feel the love: YES NO

My diaphragm feels: _____

_____

My equal breath count is: _____

My mind now is: _____

_____

I notice: _____

_____

I sense: _____

_____

I feel: _____

_____

I drop into my Daily Attunement easier each day: YES NO

The equal breath has become routine: YES NO

I am conscious of the energies/feelings/emotions of the day: YES NO

I am more aware of my breath in my daily activities: YES NO

I am less stressed: YES NO

Emotions (e- energy in motion) are arising as I am more aware of my body and breath. The buried emotions are arising and I feel:

Sad Happy Frustrated Angry Blissful Misunderstood Worried Confused Lost Ignored Grateful Overwhelmed Insecure

Journal - Day 3

Journal your emotions fully:

_____

_____

_____

_____

_____

_____

_____

_____

_____

I feel rooted/grounded: YES NO

I notice sensations in the fingers/hands: YES NO

I can visualize the Golden Light: YES NO

I can visualize the green light: YES NO

I can feel/sense the Light going through my body: YES NO

I sense the energy of Divine Love or: _____

I sense a feeling that is new to me that I cannot name: YES NO

I feel: _____

_____

I AM enjoying life more FULLY!: YES NO

Journal - Day 3

Journal - Day 3

Daily Attunement: Level 4

As a divine vessel/channel between Heaven and Earth, fully grounded and aware, you are now ready to strengthen and deepen the connection to your Higher Self, your God Self. Your inhalation is connecting you to the fourth-dimensional energies, or prana. In the previous exercise you connect with the fourth dimensional prana and you are bringing it down into this third dimensional world, and sharing it as you exhale it into this third dimensional world.

When we pray or meditate we are trying to connect with that invisible force that we may call God or Universe or Source. This connection is crucial to living what I call a full and conscious life. This so-called force or energy is within everyone. It is within every living thing including plants, animals, insects, etc. It is the energy that keeps the stars and sun and moon and planets in orbit and affects our being, our bodies, our mind. The Flower of Life, a sacred geometric shape that goes as far back as ancient Egypt, as far as we know from early sightings, depicts the interconnectedness of all living things. It represents the six days of creation.

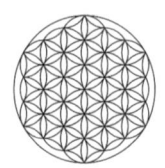

This image is believed to contain the Divine blueprint of all creation, the DNA of all living things. The blueprint is in every electron of our Beings. So within our Being, is the whole universe, and we are within every other living Being.

As a channel for the Divine you may expect to be perfect, holy, full of light. To achieve such states of Being, we use the Violet Flame, a gift of self-healing from God. The Violet flame is a cleansing and healing tool given to all humanity by God. Ascended Master St. Germain is responsible for making humanity aware of this gift and how to use it. It is recommended that you use the Violet Flame for self-healing 24/7.

To Invoke the Violet flame, out loud I invite you to state:

"Oh Violet Flame, blaze, blaze, blaze. Transmute and transform the cause, core and effect of all karma, all negative energy, and all vibrations lower than my holy Christ Self." (from Patricia Cota Robles)

When I am doing healing work, I "see" my hands vibrating the three-fold Violet Flame and as magnetized fields of energy my hands are attracting and pulling out the energies that are disrupting the life force.

Even in moments of distress, you may quickly say this invocation out loud and imagine the three-fold flame in full power!

As you now may be realizing that the Daily Attunement of our Being must affect the whole universe as we are connected to every other living thing and the blueprint for the universe is within us, let's go WITHIN to see and feel the deeper connection with our Higher Self, our God Self.

"If we simply allow our Three-Fold flame and our Holy Christ Selves to have full dominion of our four lower bodies, the intelligent elemental substance that compromises our actual cells will cooperate with us and our four lower bodies will be transformed into the perfection of our Holy Christ Self."

Patricia Diane Cota Roble, "Your Time is at Hand"

1. Repeat each of the steps as outlined in Level 3, up to step 25. This process now will be much quicker and easier.

2. As a fully connected Being, bring your awareness into your heart center and BE Still. As the holder of your Divine Blueprint and the Violet Flame, the heart radiates the qualities of Light, Love and Power. (A fuller explanation of the flame is in the next step.)

3. Visualize the Violet Flame as a three-fold flame. A sapphire blue flame is on the left, representing the Divine Masculine. A crystalline pink flame is on the right representing the Divine Feminine. The golden flame in the center is the representation of Wisdom/Christ Consciousness. With the fullness of your attention, continue this visualization. See, sense, feel the flames blazing.

4. The three-fold flame is now expanding deep within your heart, with each breath you take and guided by your intention for it to blaze, blaze, blaze. Notice, sense, the expansion of the heart area and the flame. Notice the intensity of your thoughts, intention.

The flame is your agent of Self- Healing. The flame is a gift from God, and it is the power of God within us. It is the power to transmute and transform all that is of a lower vibration than our true God Self. The violet flame transmutes the cause, core and effect of karma. Like taking a daily shower, you may cleanse and clear your auric field as needed.

Three fold flame image courtesy of Summit Lighthouse

5. Now INVOKE the power of the Violet Flame and SAY OUT LOUD:

"Oh Violet Flame, blaze, blaze, blaze. Transmute and transform the cause, core and effect of all karma, all negative energy, and all vibrations lower than my holy Christ Self."

Notice the sensations as you speak, notice the power of the words, feel energy moving throughout you.

6. Breathe, focus, and intend that the flame is blazing to its fullest intensity. Continue with the equal breathing until it feels it has reached its optimum expansion, hold it and sense it, notice.

7. Visualize the flame now overflowing from your heart into your hands. Notice the magnetic energy in your hands! Notice heat and vibrations.

8. The energy of the flame pouring into your hands is like water and you use your hands in a motion as if you are washing off, or cleansing your physical body. Sense the magnetic force in your hands as you "wash." Then shake out your hands as if throwing the energy out the window or door. Notice the hands as the energy releases. After washing the physical body layer, imagine you are washing/cleansing your etheric layer body, sensing and feeling the hands and the "body." Then your mental layer body and then the emotional layer body. With full deliberation, mindfulness, slowly you cleanse each layer. With each layer or "body" you are using your magnetized hands to clear the front, the back and right and left sides, just like cleansing your body in a shower. Notice the energies in your hands at all times.

9. Continue the three-fold/Violet flame clearing for as long as a month -- or until you are sensing the "bodies,"-- before proceeding to the next step.

The noticing, sensing and eventually "feeling" each "body" with your hands as you clear them with the Violet Flame is an ability that may develop over time. Each "body" may have its own sensations or vibrations. I invite you to deepen your Attunement to "feel" the vibratory field of each body.

To deepen the intention and focus, know that the physical body which you know well, is connected to the elemental substance of the earth.

The next layer/body is approximately 6 inches out from the physical body and that is the etheric body. That is your energy double. The etheric is the air element.

The third body is the mental layer and that is our thoughts and beliefs. The mental body is the fire element.

The next layer/body is the emotional layer. This is often considered the hardest to heal and it is the water element.

These so-called "four lower bodies" must be healed in order for us to Ascend into our true Light bodies.

Journal - Day 1

I easily visualized the Violet Flame: YES NO

I can feel/sense my heart: YES NO

I easily visualized the Violet Flame in my heart center: YES NO

My hands feel energy/tingling/heaviness/warmth/coolness: YES NO

I am more aware of situations that bother me, trigger me: YES NO

I sense/feel my diaphragm reacting to emotional situations: YES NO

Emotions are arising: YES NO

I am feeling buried emotions arising, such as:

Fearfulness   Annoyance   Joyousness   Being Energized   Positivity   Helplessness   Feeling Unimportant   Sadness   Happiness

Journal your emotions fully:

_____
_____
_____
_____
_____
_____
_____
_____
_____
_____

Journal - Day 1

The next item is being included as many students are having Images arise, inner child experiences, divine interventions. All experiences are individual and of course they represent whatever is in the student's best and highest interest/what they are ready to receive. So please no expectations, but should something arise, enjoy journaling about it!

I had a vision/message of: _____

_____

_____

I sensed an energy around me, a cool air, a warmth, a hug:

_____

_____

I heard a divine being say: _____

_____

_____

For Violet Flame healing portion:

Physical body layer I feel _____ with my hands

Etheric body layer I feel _____ with my hands

Mental body layer I feel _____ with my hands

Emotional body layer I feel _____ with my hands

Journal - Day 1

Journal - Day 1

Journal - Day 2

I easily visualized the Violet Flame: YES NO

I can feel/sense my heart: YES NO

I easily visualized the Violet Flame in my heart center: YES NO

My hands feel energy/tingling/heaviness/warmth/coolness: YES NO

I am more aware of situations that bother me, trigger me: YES NO

I sense/feel my diaphragm reacting to emotional situations: YES NO

Emotions are arising: YES NO

I am feeling buried emotions arising, such as:

Fearfulness   Annoyance   Joyousness   Being Energized   Positivity   Helplessness   Feeling Unimportant   Sadness   Happiness

Journal your emotions fully:

_____
_____
_____
_____
_____
_____
_____
_____
_____
_____
_____

Journal - Day 2

The next item is being included as many students are having Images arise, inner child experiences, divine interventions. All experiences are individual and of course they represent whatever is in the student's best and highest interest/what they are ready to receive. So please no expectations, but should something arise, enjoy journaling about it!

I had a vision/message of: _____

_____

_____

I sensed an energy around me, a cool air, a warmth, a hug:

_____

_____

I heard a divine being say: _____

_____

_____

For Violet Flame healing portion:

Physical body layer I feel _____ with my hands

Etheric body layer I feel _____ with my hands

Mental body layer I feel _____ with my hands

Emotional body layer I feel _____ with my hands

Journal - Day 2

Journal - Day 2

Journal - Day 3

I easily visualized the Violet Flame: YES NO

I can feel/sense my heart: YES NO

I easily visualized the Violet Flame in my heart center: YES NO

My hands feel energy/tingling/heaviness/warmth/coolness: YES NO

I am more aware of situations that bother me, trigger me: YES NO

I sense/feel my diaphragm reacting to emotional situations: YES NO

Emotions are arising: YES NO

I am feeling buried emotions arising, such as:

Fearfulness   Annoyance   Joyousness   Being Energized   Positivity   Helplessness   Feeling Unimportant   Sadness   Happiness

Journal your emotions fully:

_____
_____
_____
_____
_____
_____
_____
_____
_____
_____

Journal - Day 3

The next item is being included as many students are having Images arise, inner child experiences, divine interventions. All experiences are individual and of course they represent whatever is in the student's best and highest interest/what they are ready to receive. So please no expectations, but should something arise, enjoy journaling about it!

I had a vision/message of: _____

_____

_____

I sensed an energy around me, a cool air, a warmth, a hug:

_____

_____

I heard a divine being say: _____

_____

_____

For Violet Flame healing portion:

Physical body layer I feel _____ with my hands

Etheric body layer I feel _____ with my hands

Mental body layer I feel _____ with my hands

Emotional body layer I feel _____ with my hands

Journal - Day 3

Journal - Day 3

Daily Attunement: Level 5

What we say and think is the energy behind every creation. In the fourth dimension, what we think and feel IS what we create and can manifest almost instantly. This IS powerful! We must consciously choose our words and thoughts every moment. What is said out loud has even more power and is heard by the angelic realm as well as by our four lower bodies. Our auric field absorbs energy, and words are energy. So invocations, intentions, mantras, and prayers are tools used in self-healing and in connecting with the Higher Consciousness. In the visualizations of these attunements it is important to use the full power of your mind, your full intent, and believe in the end result. The three-fold Violet Flame is your focus of Light, Love and Power!

The blue ray, the divine masculine, represents God's power and God's Will. It is considered the first ray of Ascension and is also associated with Archangel Michael. The pink ray, the divine feminine, represents God's unconditional love and it is the third ray of Ascension, associated with Archangel Chamuel. The yellow/golden ray is the second ray of Ascension and it is the wisdom ray, or the ray associated with the Light of Consciousness. It is also associated with Archangel Jophiel.

As we seek to activate the qualities of the divine masculine and feminine within, the key is to also balance energies in our auric field and in our heart center. These energies are not based on the gender of our physical bodies. They are the balancing of the Godly energies from which we were created and yet may have been diminished or lost when we entered the earthly plane, whether at the time of the "fall" or in each earthly incarnation. The power is in visualizing these rays and intently focusing on assimilating their qualities into our auric field and light body.

Now to implement level 5 - to balance the Divine Masculine and Feminine vibrations, continue from Level 4, and:

1. Inhale and bring your focus to the point of light, the Great Central Sun, about 12 inches above your head, and on the exhale visualize a beautiful sapphire blue ray coming down and through the left side of your body, all the way into the earth. On the next inhale imagine a crystalline pink ray coming up from the center of the earth, up and through the right side of your body, all the way up to the brilliant point of light.

On the next exhale repeat the process with the blue ray coming down the left side of the body into the earth, and on the inhalation visualize the pink ray coming up the right side of the body all the way to the point of light. Keep this going until you feel balanced on the left and right sides. Sense, feel, notice the vibration of both these rays. Note, sense the right side of the body versus the left side. Note the feeling of balance in your body.

2. Once you feel balanced, the next time you reach the point of light above your head, exhale and visualize the golden ray of wisdom coming down the center of your body in the front, all the way into the earth. On the inhalation visualize the golden ray going up the back of your body, all the way up to the point of light above your head.

Repeat this process with the exhale sending the golden light down the front of the body and the inhalation bringing it up the back of the body, all the way up to the point of
light above your head. Keep this going until you feel balanced and whole. Sensing, feeling, noticing.

3. BE still.

Journal - Day 1

I easily visualized the three-fold Violet Flame: YES   NO

I sense/feel the Sapphire Blue flame descending down the left side of my body: YES   NO

I sense/feel the Crystalline Pink ray rising up the right side of my body: YES   NO

I sense/feel the Golden Ray descending the front of my body and ascending the backside of my body: YES   NO

Overall I feel: _____

_____

_____

_____

_____

_____

_____

_____

I had a vision/message of: _____

_____

_____

_____

_____

_____

_____

Journal - Day 1

Journal - Day 2

I easily visualized the three-fold Violet Flame: YES   NO

I sense/feel the Sapphire Blue flame descending down the left side of my body: YES   NO

I sense/feel the Crystalline Pink ray rising up the right side of my body: YES   NO

I sense/feel the Golden Ray descending the front of my body and ascending the backside of my body: YES   NO

Overall I feel: _____

_____

_____

_____

_____

_____

_____

I had a vision/message of: _____

_____

_____

_____

_____

_____

_____

Journal - Day 2

Journal - Day 3

I easily visualized the three-fold Violet Flame: YES   NO

I sense/feel the Sapphire Blue flame descending down the left side of my body: YES   NO

I sense/feel the Crystalline Pink ray rising up the right side of my body: YES   NO

I sense/feel the Golden Ray descending the front of my body and ascending the backside of my body: YES   NO

Overall I feel: _____

_____

_____

_____

_____

_____

_____

I had a vision/message of: _____

_____

_____

_____

_____

_____

_____

Journal - Day 3

Daily Attunement: Level 6

Sacred and Holy AM I. One with your Father/ Mother God. The pinnacle, the point of divine manifestation!

You are now vibrating possibly in the 4th or 5th dimension. Sensing, noticing, how this new relationship feels and allowing it to BE your new way of living in the 3rd dimensional world.

"HU" is a chant that opens the channels to higher consciousness. Hu is a divine love song to God.

I discovered this chant while in Egypt in the Pyramid of Giza in the King's chamber. This sacred sound was suddenly billowing from my mouth. It felt as if the apex of the chamber opened up, the capstone slid away and the whole universe appeared and the light shone in. Now mind you, at the time I had no idea where this chant came from, I had never heard it before. Months later at home I was awoken by this sound, but thought it was someone playing my singing bowls. Later in the day I happened upon an Eckankar meeting and they started chanting. The chant was HU! This chant is believed to raise our consciousness and bring us closer to God.

Balanced and whole, you are a clear and open channel. Continue from level 5 and:

1. With arms up to the sky, chant "HU" to further open your divine connection. Chant "HU" out loud and notice, sense, the spaciousness being created above the crown chakra.

2. From deep within, on your next inhalation, raise your consciousness, your focus, to a point of brilliant white light about 12 inches above your head. This is the Light of your I AM Consciousness, the Great Central Sun.

3. As you hold the inhalation, intone the mantra, I AM THAT I AM.

4. Then as you exhale out the mouth, visualize that brilliant white light becoming a blazing ball of explosive, radiating light that descends upon your crown chakra and down through your auric field. (The radiating light may also appear as a golden white light.) Your whole Being is bathed in this light that we call the Christ Consciousness. (Please note this term is referencing a state of Being, a state of consciousness, not the person known as Jesus Christ. Many have reached this state of consciousness and we often refer to them as Ascended Masters.)

5. Every cell of your Being is being activated by the Light of God.

6. Repeat steps 2 thru 5, at least 5 more times, minimum.

7. BE Still. Let Go and let God.

8. Set the intention that you hold this high vibration, and stay aligned with the Higher Consciousness moment to moment.

9. Notice, sense, feel, see, and KNOW that your whole Being is being permeated with this high vibration of God Consciousness, as you float back into the heart.

Passion, desire, adoration, and a thirst for the coming of the Divine into your life elicits a response from the Divine! You are a creator and a co-creator with God. At this point you can start to realign and redesign your life.

Journal - Day 1

I notice, sense, feel, my four lower bodies are changing in vibration: YES   NO

I feel the energy of each lower body as I cleanse them with the Violet Flame: YES   NO

I feel the raising of my vibratory field: YES   NO

I feel my auric field expanding: YES   NO

I easily visualize the white light and the golden blazing ball of light: YES   NO

I sense, feel a Higher Presence: YES   NO

I notice I live more from my heart center: YES   NO

I am calm, peaceful, fulfilled and aligned: YES   NO

I feel a shift in consciousness: YES   NO

I am living more purposefully: YES   NO

Journal - Day 1

Journal - Day 2

I notice, sense, feel, my four lower bodies are changing in vibration: YES   NO

I feel the energy of each lower body as I cleanse them with the Violet Flame: YES   NO

I feel the raising of my vibratory field: YES   NO

I feel my auric field expanding: YES   NO

I easily visualize the white light and the golden blazing ball of light: YES   NO

I sense, feel a Higher Presence: YES   NO

I notice I live more from my heart center: YES   NO

I am calm, peaceful, fulfilled and aligned: YES   NO

I feel a shift in consciousness: YES   NO

I am living more purposefully: YES   NO

Journal - Day 2

Journal - Day 3

I notice, sense, feel, my four lower bodies are changing in vibration: YES   NO

I feel the energy of each lower body as I cleanse them with the Violet Flame: YES   NO

I feel the raising of my vibratory field: YES   NO

I feel my auric field expanding: YES   NO

I easily visualize the white light and the golden blazing ball of light: YES   NO

I sense, feel a Higher Presence: YES   NO

I notice I live more from my heart center: YES   NO

I am calm, peaceful, fulfilled and aligned: YES   NO

I feel a shift in consciousness: YES   NO

I am living more purposefully: YES   NO

Journal - Day 3

Part 2

In this uplifting process of Reconnecting to your Divine Self and Resurrecting yourself back to life, you also have started the process of Realigning and Redesigning your Being. KNOW that energy flows where your attention goes.

As you have been focusing your energy on connection with Source, you are realigning your Light body and getting clearer, more precise information, aha's, and messages or signs that have been appearing on the golden path way. You are tapping into a higher vibrational consciousness and thus rising above the lower vibrations of this earthly plane. You are lining up with a better "team," ascended masters and guides, with more inspiration and intuition, from the Higher Consciousness. You are Attuning! You are realigning your energy/light body and thus it is attracting higher vibrations according to your new vibratory field.

One key ingredient in realigning is the changing or refocusing of our thoughts and beliefs. What is real? Depending on our age, we may or may not have started to assess what we feel is Truth versus how we were raised. Are we living like robots and not thinking for ourselves? Do you follow your heart? Do you delve into subjects, current or historical, to determine what feels right to you? Many people just go along with the mass consciousness.

You are changing! This process has awakened you to think for yourself, to feel, to sense and be more open and aware of the information coming through your higher consciousness in various forms and ways. You are an individual and yet you are part of the whole of humanity. You have your individual consciousness and you are part of the collective consciousness, as we are all One.

Realigning can also mean taking different steps, going in a different direction or refocusing your energies. You might now be refining your sense of Self and what you are really on this earth for. How do you best use your skills, your gifts and talents? What is your Soul's purpose?

Isn't this part of self-healing? Finding our true Self, our purpose in life, our "Why" and then using it to help humanity as well as ourselves?

"The divine Christ lives in the heart of men and women as divine love and passionate service to the divine light irrespective of religious persuasion. The divine light is whatever form we believe it to be – whether that be Allah, or God, or Krishna or Shiva or a guru or the universe, or anything else for that matter. Provided that it is love you are serving, then the Christ Consciousness or unconditional divine wisdom, love or power that the holy Mother seeks to awaken with us, can live in you."

From: Mother Mary Oracle Cards
Card #15 Our Lady of the Sacred Son

Chapter 4

Tools For Self-Healing

I have many tools to further assist the realigning and redesigning process, the last two steps in my Divine Matrix healing method. As always, sense, feel, intuit what speaks to you and give the tool(s) your fullest engagement. I also suggest trying new tools every so often and, even though you may resist, know that resistance is often a sign that it is something you actually need to do to push you to the next level. What is uncomfortable will help you grow.

1. Call back and erase – this has to do with thoughts and things said out loud. In your new state of awareness/consciousness be more mindful of what you think and say. Is it True? Is it of a negative or limiting nature? Is it a false belief, a fear or a worry? When it is of the lower vibration, you immediately say out loud (power of the spoken word):

"I call back and erase that statement."

Then, out loud say the exact opposite of the statement you just thought or said. Say it in present tense and ideally start with, "I AM", the phrase of the Christ Consciousness.

For example:

I am so afraid of making the wrong decision.
Change to: *I AM choosing what is right for me at the moment.*

I don't have enough money to live as I wish.
Change to: *I AM God abundant and I always have all that I need.*

This is a vibrational tool. We said before your energy body absorbs all that you say and think as well as from others. What you focus on is what you create, what you will "see." The more positive you focus your thoughts the higher will your vibration stay and you will attract higher vibrational experiences. When you focus on the positive you will start taking actions that support the new statement or belief and the creation will start manifesting in this dimension, in your view of the world. The negative or limiting thoughts can block you from seeing what is real and what is right in front of you. Often we say, we have put up a wall and we just can't see what is right in front of our own eyes.

You probably already know that the negative and limiting beliefs may come from traumatic experiences, hurtful words, misunderstood words and responses. With each breath hopefully we are taking a new look at ourselves and freeing the trauma from our body. Many say it is not this simple, to just think positively. I agree. We need to think new thoughts, those that are truth, and often we need actual help releasing the trauma from our body with healing modalities like the ones mentioned earlier. The beliefs, the self judgment and criticisms have a hold on us that may not be conscious. Often the trauma is buried. If we don't see it or feel it, how do we release it? You guessed it--it may be in your face by the way others respond to you. Yes, others often mirror your own beliefs and attitudes. What you see in another that triggers you is IN you!

I invite you to start a personal journal, expanding on all that you have already discovered through the Daily Attunements, to this next level of self-healing. Journaling helps you to see the patterns and the progress.

2. The "mirror" is another tool that usually we need help with in the beginning.

Example, you say/think: Susie is so critical and judgmental.

Turn it around and say: *I AM so critical and judgmental.*

I suggest you feel this in your body as you say it out loud three times slowly. As you say it each time, notice, feel, sense and breathe! The mirror can show you aspects of yourself that are wonderful, exciting, special or it may show you aspects of yourself that secretly you really don't like. It is believed that you cannot see something in another person unless it is in you as well. This means you are familiar with the energy, it touches a chord within you, and it may even trigger an emotional response.

Journal Prompts:
Where did you feel it in your body?
What did you feel in your body?
What emotions arose?
What thoughts arose?
Is it True?

This is a powerful self-awareness tool. You are being honest with Self as your body tells you the Truth. This will help you catch the negative/limiting thoughts and turn them around. Call those thoughts back, cleanse and clear them and then say the opposite out loud!

I invite you to include the mirror experiences in your journal as well. This may be a wowza, seeing your thoughts and beliefs and how what you see in others may really be an aspect of yourself. You got it! It is easy and powerful! You are the healer! All the answers are WITHIN YOU!

The biggest complaint I hear is that this is a fulltime job! So let's clean out the negativity, the limiting beliefs, the trash so to speak. Let's fill our auric field with the high vibration of Light and Love from God. "The spirit of God moved upon the face of the waters," it says in the Bible. Spirit is breath! Water represents emotions. The breath releases the emotions!

Know, when your field is clear you are more receptive to the information from above and you will be guided to achieving that which you are seeking, especially if it is in your best and highest interest.

3. Mantras and Affirmations – Mantras have been used since the beginning of time. You may be familiar with "OM," or "Om Namah Shiva," or other sacred statements given by Gurus and Ascended Masters. For many more powerful mantras/invocations/affirmations for the Violet Flame and

Ascended Masters, I invite you to connect with the Summit Lighthouse.org. As you sensed with the Violet Flame invocation we used in this book, these invocations are very high vibration. Also popular in the last 20 years or so are positive affirmations. Louise Hay is an author and well known spiritual guru of positive, mind/body affirmations as healing tools. She states the mind/body thought that is the "probable cause" of an ailment and then she gives the new thought pattern – the affirmation to use repetitively. You can see this goes hand-in-hand with the previous tools. The "sound" when these are spoken out loud, reverberates into your energy field as we keep repeating.

The power of the spoken word is relatable to God/Source, for God "spoke" to and through the prophets. Is that the tiny, quiet voice within that you hear when you BE STILL?

The mantras and affirmations, along with the breath and focus and intent, can create a shift in your energy body and help to raise your vibration. The shift creates feelings of peace, calm, quiet, knowing, freedom, and whatever else you have already listed in your journals. Keep up the good work! It is working!

4. Gratitude – I sincerely invite you to start and end each day by writing down what you are grateful for at that moment. In the morning, after recording your dreams and maybe just before starting your Daily Attunements, writing what you are grateful for sets the tone for the day. It brings you into a state of mindfulness as you look within, stop and feel and notice all the good around you. Ending your day the same way creates a beautiful state of peace and the heart fills with gratitude for the day, people, God, nature, etc. Your gratitudes may be written in a journal.

5. I choose – Another great morning activity. Start each sentence that you write with "I choose" and fill in the blank. What you choose to focus on is what you will create and the thought and solidifying it on paper will inform the cells of your body and your auric field. You may wish to keep this with you during the day should you need help refocusing where your thoughts are going. Obviously I invite you to choose positive thoughts that you truly wish to create and make a reality in your life and those around you.

6. Toning – similar but different to the mantras and affirmations. Toning is about sounds that we use to vibrate our chakras, our energy body. The HU I mentioned earlier is very powerful. Also, many chakra practices teach the "sound" for each chakra for you to intone and awaken or balance that energy center. As always, the key is to feel in, deep within, notice, sense the vibrations within and without.

7. Hand mudras – The Christian prayer pose of hands together and all fingers touching can be considered an ancient hand mudra. In our Daily Attunement exercises the energy is running through your fingers, especially when you have reached up to the heavenly realms and called in your I AM presence. Each finger represents one of the elements. The little finger is earth, ring finger is water, middle finger is fire, index finger is air and the thumb is ether. The same is true for your toes and we use these corresponding energies in Acupuncture and Reflexology to understand the balance or imbalances of one's being.

The mudras, also known as hand yoga exercises, are like affirmations as you focus on an energy or a new thought pattern with breath and a mantra. You are running different currents of energy flow through the fingers into your body for self-healing. The healing can be for body, mind or spirit.

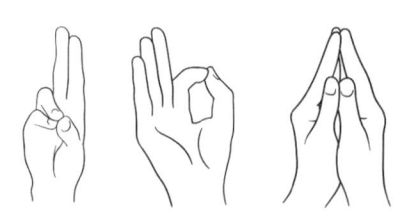

Example: A common mudra for those practicing yoga and meditation is: hands on your lap. Thumb and little finger are touching one another, on each hand. This is a grounding mudra as the little finger represents earth and the thumb is the ethers – higher consciousness. So you are connecting the two! As always, noticing, sensing, feeling, the vibrations within and without body. I invite you to do this in your daily attunement breathing exercises.

8. Body positions – I already mentioned the poses for your Daily Attunement exercises. I also like to use body positions with affirmations that I have been given by spirit. They make a statement physically and verbally, as of course I say the affirmation out loud.

Example: I AM THAT I AM. That is the affirmation I use to connect with the higher consciousness, with God, my true God Self, as you experienced in the exercises. The body poses are as follows:

I = Legs together and arms straight up with hands clasped together.

AM = Keep arms and hands as so and move right leg out to the side.

THAT = Bring right leg back in and brings arms down to shoulder height and out like a cross.

I = Legs stay together and arms come back up and clasp hands together.

AM= Keep arms and hands as so and move left leg out to the side.

Notice, the "I" is like a straight arrow pointing up to heaven. Notice the sensations in the body.

The "AM" is like a pyramid or mountain shape, or an A. Notice the power and maybe grounding energy in this stance.

The "That" is like a cross, the cross roads or intersection between heaven and earth. Notice the sensations and possible emotions that arise.

The "I" again is the arrow pointing up to heaven. Notice the energy flowing from your fingers up into the heavens and down into your fingers from the heavens.

The "AM" is again the pyramid, the mountain, the A. Notice the confirmation of this stance, the strength in the statement as a whole.

So, I AM the Mountain. I AM the Cross. I AM the Pyramid. These are all symbolic of power, healing, life and resurrection and so much more. The poses also remind me a little of the Warrior poses in yoga as they ground and stabilize me.

9. Signs and Symbols – I teach a class on following the signs and symbols from Source. I call them the stepping stones, the bread crumbs that lead us on the path to our Divine Self, to our I AM Presence. This is about living consciously. Remember I said through the use of the Daily Attunement exercises you will be more aware, more conscious, more in tune with life, with God. Signs are often found in nature, purely God's expressions. The signs may be birds, animals, flowers, trees, fish, insects, sun, moon, clouds, etc. A sign may be something unusual you find on the ground, or a sound you hear. A sign is something that catches your attention, elicits a feeling, or a response from your being. It touches you and makes you take notice. Every so-called sign or symbol has a meaning. To learn what the usual meaning is, just ask on your phone, "What is the spiritual symbolism of _____?"

At the same time I invite you to notice, sense what is going on when you see the sign or symbol. What are you thinking, or saying and feeling? What is happening IN the moment that you saw the sign or symbol? This is important as it appeared for you at that time for a reason. There are no mistakes or coincidences, everything is for a reason. I will also give you a great resource for animals at the end of the book as the key is to "work" with the message you just received. What is it inviting you to see about yourself or your life? I invite you to always journal these signs and symbols as well, as you will start to see patterns and your progression on this journey of life!

Signs and messages offer great journaling opportunities. Actually, they are a MUST in my opinion.

Example: I found 22 pennies on the ground one day as I was preparing my notes for a class on signs and symbols. So I looked up the spiritual meaning of finding pennies. Then I looked up the spiritual meaning of the number 22 and the number two. Of course you can find multiple meanings and you will start to find the "sites" that feel right to you. Then I worked with the messages and applied it to what was going on in the moment and in my current life. The pennies definitely were a message about going forward and what is to come. The number 2 is the master builder/creator.

10. Dreams – Dreams are also a sign or a message from the unconscious. I recommend you keep a separate dream journal.

Keep this by your bed and before getting out of bed write down your dreams with as much details and feelings as possible. They are an indicator of what is going on at the moment. If you really keep the journals and stay conscious you will find that the dreams probably are paralleling some of the signs and messages you are receiving. Isn't that crazy! It feels like Source/Universe/God has a hand in all this, doesn't it? I love living consciously!

There are many sources of dream interpretation and, again, you can research the meaning on your phone. I happen to be drawn to Carl Jung dream therapy methods and symbolism, as he is the "father" of Archetypal energies and understanding of the unconscious, in my limited understanding. I am not equipped to teach you the methods here so I will list books and sites at the end of this book.

11. Mandala – sacred circles- symbols of healing and wholeness

"In its most elevated form, the sacred circle mirrors an illumined state of consciousness through a symbolic pattern - making the invisible visible." -Judith Cornell, Pg. 2 of "Mandala"

Like a dream, you open the door to divine energies and to your own psychological self when you work with mandalas. This is an art form used in many hospitals as it is calming, relaxing and can help one to strengthen the will to heal, and it comes from within. The creation of your own mandala is a powerful process indeed. For those wishing something simpler, one may purchase the mandala coloring books that can assist you with coming into a meditative, deep, spiritual place.

12. Golden Pyramid - a sacred geometric shape that is known for its healing element and can be used as a protective shield of God's Light. When you are grounded and connected as you have learned

to do through the Daily Attunement exercises, visualize a golden pyramid coming down and around you from above, all the way to the ground. You are the central channel of the pyramid. You are fully protected in this golden light of sacred geometry. No vibration lower than yours may enter your field and you may state this out loud as you engage with the energy. For those of you who are empathic, you may need to use this any time you are encountering another person. For added protection you may also add mirrors to the outside walls of the pyramid. Sensing a negative energy, or one that has triggered you in the past, imagine the mirrors reflecting the other person's energy back to them, with love. You may stay present, holding space, and yet not taking on their energies. Sacred and holy vibration.

13. Flower of Life - this is an ancient symbol of the six days of creation. It is a powerful manifestation tool. I suggest using a plain version of this image to meditate upon. Focus upon the most center point, what I like to call the eye of the needle. Focus, stare and blink as little as possible. Breathe, stare, let go and see the divine images arising from this pattern of all living things. Let life come alive before your eyes.

Chapter 5

Redesign Your Life

You are on the path and there is no turning back! Your light body is aligned with the Higher Consciousness and you will fine tune it daily as you focus on creating the new you, the True you, the Real you. You have opened the door to higher consciousness and you are living life fully!

Congratulations!

All along life has been changing and you are not the same person as when you started this program. In fact, you have been redesigning since day one. Every cell of your being started shifting on day one.

Every time you do the breathing you are inviting in Spirit, the breath of God! Every time you breathe deep and connect to those rays of Divine light, the lost parts of Self, you are resurrecting yourself!

Take a deep breath now, hold it, exhale it and leave it out...

Take a deeper breath now, hold it, exhale it deeper, leave it out...

Take a deep breath and bring your focus up to the Great Central Sun, hold it as you intone the mantra, "I AM THAT I AM," great exhale out the mouth, leave it out and drift out, way out, upon the sea of consciousness, God consciousness... drift, let go, let go into Oneness, let go into serenity, let GO into Nothingness... let GO into God's vast, loving embrace. Let GO, BE STILL, BE ONE.

Now what? Are the messages, intuitions, synchronicities and aha's now daily or possibly hourly? Who is talking to you? Where are all these energies coming from? Have they been here all along? As you focus on being aligned, tuned in and connected to Source/God, Source/God IS responding! Your messages and intentions are getting through the sea of consciousness and your call is being answered. Are you hearing and answering God's "call"?

Change is sometimes not easy and many of us resist change. We seem to fear it and believe it is not a good thing. That is not Truth. Change is the only constant in life and when you float on the golden lazy river, it will take you to exactly where you need to go. Of course it is a journey, maybe with twists and turns, and with some challenges and opportunities. We learn, we grow and this is what we call life.

If something is not working in your best and highest interest, the Universe may give you a sign, or throw a monkey wrench in your current situation, somehow changing things up. It is important to be aware of the signs and messages, because if we keep missing the guidance, sooner or later the Universe may give us a BIG wake up call. It is like the Universe starts with signs and messages, eventually leads to a tap if we are not listening, then maybe to a scare, and if we still don't listen maybe to something that really grabs our attention, and not necessarily in a good way. Often things, i.e.: relationships, businesses, religions, government, economy, and even our bodies may need to totally fall apart in order to be rebuilt or redesigned. I'd like to invite you to continue your good work and avoid any dramatic wake-up calls by choosing to live consciously and take this step to follow the breadcrumbs from the Universe and deepen the resolve to redesign your life.

The "call" is what many consider a "knowing"; a sensing of energy moving through their whole Being. A direct call from God certainly feels special. I remember thinking, ME God? Really, you want ME to do what? I am not special, why me? I don't have those skills, why are you asking me? Oh my God, this is actually something I have dreamed of my whole life! Is this real? Have you been hearing me my whole life? Is this what I have been searching for, waiting for? Is this real God?

Of course all this "head stuff" elicits a response from God! "Stop talking," God says, "Let us take over! Trust me, it will all work out. Trust me! Be patient and just listen. We wish to talk to you each day. It is time, we need your attention and devotion. We will guide you, let go." This is what God has said to me, more than once!

This book, Daily Attunement, has the accompaniment of videos showing classes for the breathwork that are guided by me and of course the angelic realm occasionally pops in. These videos are to assist you in addition to the step by step process in this book. As this is being written other self-healing related videos are being planned and produced and will be available to you.

I AM listening. I AM trusting. I AM following the signs, messages, visions and dreams, the best I can. I AM asking daily for continued guidance and unconditional love. I AM immersed in the Sea of Divine Consciousness.

Bless you all, for WE ARE ONE!

Journal

1. Review your journals for patterns emerging. What are the key elements in those patterns? The key elements may be: emotional patterns arising, patterns of life struggles, numbers that repeat, animals that keep calling for your attention, sensations/feelings, negative or limiting thoughts, fears/worries, changes in relationships, health issues or job issues that repeat themselves, and so on.

2. Take a deep breath in, ascend up to the Great Central Sun, and now imagine you are looking down from the Great Central Sun. Ask your Higher Self, Higher Consciousness to show you what these patterns are truly about. Often you will get insights from childhood or earlier time frames and you will notice that an old event is being triggered, remembered in your cellular body.

3. Journal the emotions arising, and the remembrances. "See" how what is current is really about the past! It is not about the details, it is about the emotions.

_____

_____

_____

_____

_____

_____

_____

_____

_____

_____

It is no mistake or coincidence if you see a sign or message that occurs multiple times. It is a sign! If you don't pay attention, the Universe increases the intensity of the messages in various ways. I call that a wake-up call. It is the Universe saying, hello, are you listening to me? Do not dismiss anything. Do not dismiss a feeling, or a sensing, or a gut reaction or what feels like a "knowing". Something is arising and your higher Self is calling you to pay attention in the moment. This is why the journal is a very important tool. There is no way you will remember all the signs, messages, dreams while going about your daily activities and work.

The opportunity to experience Self, God, is yours and yours alone as you abide in this beautiful, glowing heart center, allowing the Christ Consciousness to awaken within. No set time, no rules, no expectations. Opening to embrace the experience in whatever form it arises each time. You always get what you need at the moment.

Bless you and congratulations on beginning the Journey of Daily Attunement, a journey into our True Self. This is just a starting point dear ones. Once you are fully grounded and connected, aware and seeking, then the universe is yours to explore, the universe is at your fingertips and footsteps. Open up, connect up and you will be stunned by all the messages God sends you.

Below I have referenced some of the many great gurus, teachers and authors that I have studied with or that, through their writings, have influenced my spiritual journey since about the age of 11. I apologize for any I may have missed; this has been a lifelong journey, many lifetimes, in fact, and with many more to come.

Let's Stay Connected!

I offer classes for the Daily Attunements. To register please email me and the listing/dates will be sent to you. Early on a great set of videos were recorded showing me guiding a class through the Daily Attunements. Of course Higher Self came in and added wording, visualizations, and floated us through the process. The videos will be a great aid for those who are more auditory and the book is great for all. To connect to the videos we produced with this Daily Attunement process, scan the code below.

I am also available for private healing sessions, spiritual coaching, and guidance in person or on Zoom. I offer classes and retreats for many spiritual topics and spiritual development.

I meet you where you are at, assist you in aligning with your Higher Self and together we co-create along with the will of God!

I invite you to email me at: solewoman9@gmail.com to be put on our email list. Please specify your interest(s) in the email subject line:

Private session, Retreats, Classes, Meditations, Spiritual guidance, Announcements of Books and Videos or you may ask for any other guidance. Or text/call 781-258-9942.

Address: Heart and Soul Holistic Healing Center, 130 Massapoag Ave, Sharon, MA

Website: www.heartandsoulholistic.com

Business Phone: 781-784-1955

Cell Phone: 781-258-9942

Email: solewoman9@gmail.com

FB: @TheSoleWoman

YouTube: Light Divine with Barbara Ann Strassman – Meditations with channeled messages

Soon to be published: The Way of (God's) Love – A journey of messages and visions and how God plays a key role in our lives.

References

These are some of the many great gurus, teachers, and schools with whom I trained, was initiated, or had visions and messages from. Also listed are authors and organizations that I have been affiliated with for many years. Along the way I have developed my own healing practice, my abilities to channel, and then by divine intervention I was guided to my own healing method, the Divine Matrix. This channeled information was given to me in various steps, over time and through various means. After seeing its profound healing effect, it was The Tibetan, Djwal Khul, that asked me to teach this healing method. That story is in my next book!

Master Kirpal Singh
Sant Ajaib Singh Ji
Maharishi Mahesh Yogi - Transcendental Meditation
Paramahansa Yogananda
Sri Ramana Maharshi
Sri Aurobindo
Mata Amritanandamayi - Amma the Hugging Saint

Virginia Francis Shippee – healer, a divine channel, including automatic writing. She also is my mother and I am so grateful to her for all the books she gave me at a very young age: Madame Blavatsky, Edgar Cayce and many others in the esoteric and mystical realms.

Rev. Richard Shippee - My brother and a Jungian Dream Analyst. I am grateful to him for years of dream guidance, love and support.

A.R.E. – Edgar Cayce, the Sleeping Prophet

Summit Lighthouse – Ascended Masters, including St. Germaine and the Violet Flame decrees

Theosophical Society – Books and teachings channeled by Madame Blavatsky

Lucis Trust - Books by Alice Bailey a channel for Djwal Khul, known as The Tibetan and as DK.

Author, spiritual teacher: Gregg Braden

Author, spiritual teacher: Patricia Cota Robles – Era of Peace

Author, spiritual teacher: Eckhart Tolle

Author, spiritual teacher, modern day mystic, theologian: Cynthia Bourgeault

Author, spiritual teacher, modern day mystic: Andrew Harvey

Marcia Hood, my Craniosacral/Myofascial Teacher/guide for several years, alternative physical therapist and mentor

Reiki Training Level 1, 2 with Patricia Warren

Reflexology training (over 400 hours) with various schools local in US and internationally

Last but not least, the many guides and ascended masters that I have channeled.

Reference Book: "Healing Mudras, Yoga for Your Hands" by Sabrina Mesko

A great book reference for signs and symbols is Animal Speak by Ted Andrews

My deepest gratitude to Andrew Harvey, author, sacred activist, mystic and scholar. Thank you for your divine insights, awareness and the message to write this small book, that you so strongly felt humanity needed.

I am ever so grateful to Jesse Dufault of Blackstone Video group. We all loved working with Jesse.

Many heartfelt thanks and blessings to my divine feminine book team; Maggie Kuhn and Renee Scheer and to Jana Katz, photographer.

Made in the USA
Columbia, SC
26 March 2024